HOLLYWOOD

AMERICAN CITIES

LOS ANGELES

Lily Erlic

LET'S READ
AV²
BY WEIGL™
ADDED VALUE · AUDIO VISUAL

Go to www.av2books.com, and enter this book's unique code.

BOOK CODE

AVP22763

AV² by Weigl brings you media enhanced books that support active learning.

AV² provides enriched content that supplements and complements this book. Weigl's AV² books strive to create inspired learning and engage young minds in a total learning experience.

Your AV² Media Enhanced books come alive with...

Audio
Listen to sections of the book read aloud.

Video
Watch informative video clips.

Embedded Weblinks
Gain additional information for research.

Try This!
Complete activities and hands-on experiments.

Key Words
Study vocabulary, and complete a matching word activity.

Quizzes
Test your knowledge.

Slide Show
View images and captions, and prepare a presentation.

... and much, much more!

Published by AV² by Weigl
350 5th Avenue, 59th Floor   New York, NY 10118
Website: www.av2books.com

Library of Congress Cataloging-in-Publication Data

Names: Erlic, Lily, author.
Title: Los Angeles / Lily Erlic.
Description: New York, NY : AV2 by Weigl, [2017] l Series: American cities l
  Audience: Grades K-3. l
Identifiers: LCCN 2017049439 (print) l LCCN 2017049496 (ebook) l ISBN
  9781489673046 (Multi User ebook) l ISBN 9781489673039 (hardcover : alk.
  paper) l ISBN 9781489677655 (softcover)
Subjects: LCSH: Los Angeles (Calif.)--Juvenile literature.
Classification: LCC F869.L84 (ebook) l LCC F869.L84 E75 2017 (print) l DDC
  979.4/94--dc23
LC record available at https://lccn.loc.gov/2017049439

Printed in the United States of America in Brainerd, Minnesota
1 2 3 4 5 6 7 8 9 0 22 21 20 19 18

032018
150318

Editor: Heather Kissock   Designer: Ana María Vidal

Weigl acknowledges Getty Images, Alamy, Newscom, Shutterstock, and iStock as the primary image suppliers for this title.

Contents

Get to Know
Los Angeles

4

Los Angeles is the biggest city in the state of California. It is known as the "Entertainment Capital of the World." Many movies and television shows are made here, in a part of the city called Hollywood.

Map of California

United States Map

Alaska Hawai'i

Golden Gate Bridge,
San Francisco

SACRAMENTO ●

Pacific Ocean

Yosemite
National Park

NEVADA

CALIFORNIA

Death Valley
National Park

ARIZONA

MAP LEGEND
- ☆ Los Angeles
- ● Capital City
- ▬ California
- ▬ United States
- ▬ Mexico
- ▬ Water

N

SCALE 0 —— 60 Miles

LOS ANGELES ☆

San Diego Zoo,
San Diego

6

Where Is Los Angeles?

Los Angeles is in the south part of California. It is 386 miles south of California's capital city, Sacramento. You can get there from Los Angeles by taking the I-5 highway.

There are many other places to visit in California. You can use a road map to plan a trip. Which roads could you take from Los Angeles to these other places? How long might it take you to get to each place?

TRAVELING CALIFORNIA
Los Angeles to San Francisco 382 miles
Los Angeles to Yosemite National Park 279 miles
Los Angeles to Death Valley National Park 258 miles
Los Angeles to San Diego 120 miles

Climate

Los Angeles is a sunny city. Summer days are hot and mostly dry. Winter is cooler and has more rainy days.

Fall brings the Santa Ana winds to the city. These winds are hot and strong. They can uproot trees during a storm. In the spring, many wildflowers bloom.

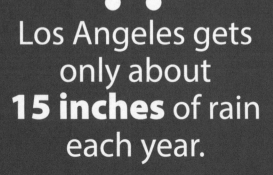

Los Angeles gets only about **15 inches** of rain each year.

Population and Geography

About 4 million people live in Los Angeles. Another 14 million people live in the area around the city. Los Angeles is one of the fastest growing cities in the United States.

Los Angeles sits on the coast of the Pacific Ocean. The San Gabriel Mountains are northeast of the city. The Los Angeles River runs through the city's center.

Many Peoples

Aboriginal Peoples lived in the Los Angeles area long before anyone else. In 1781, a group of settlers began to build a town there. They named it "The Town of Our Lady the Queen of Angels."

Over time, other people began to move to the town. Many came from the eastern United States. Today, people from many different places live in the city.

The **first group of settlers** was made up of **14 families** from northern **Mexico**.

Tourism

People often come to Los Angeles to spend time at the theme parks in the area. These include Disneyland, California Adventure, and Universal Studios Hollywood. Each park offers visitors unique rides, food, and shows.

The Hollywood Walk of Fame is another fun place to visit. There are many stars on this sidewalk. Each star has the name of a famous person on it.

There are more than **2,600 stars** on the **Hollywood Walk of Fame**.

Sports

Los Angeles has eight major sports teams. The Clippers, Lakers, and Sparks play basketball. The Kings play hockey. All of these teams use Staples Center for their home games.

The Dodgers are the city's main baseball team. They play in Dodger Stadium. The Rams and the Chargers play football. The Galaxy play soccer.

Economy

Tourism is important to the Los Angeles economy. In 2017 alone, more than 48 million people visited the city. While there, they spent money on hotels, food, and souvenirs.

Los Angeles is also a center for trade. Every day, goods are shipped to and from the city. Many of these goods travel by ship through the city's port.

The Port of Los Angeles is the **busiest port** in the **United States**.

Los Angeles Timeline

8,000 years ago
Aboriginal Peoples
live in the
Los Angeles area.

1842
Gold is found in the
Los Angeles area.

1887
Hollywood is
founded.

1781
People from Mexico build a
settlement on the land now
known as Los Angeles.

1907
The Port of Los Angeles is founded.

1999
Staples Center completes construction.

1928
The Los Angeles Municipal Airport opens. It later becomes Los Angeles International Airport, or LAX.

2016
The Wizarding World of Harry Potter opens at Universal Studios Hollywood.

Things to Do in Los Angeles

Hollywood Sign
Taking a picture of the 45-foot-tall Hollywood sign is a must for most visitors.

Griffith Park Observatory
People come here to learn more about the Sun, Moon, and stars. They can even view them through the observatory's many telescopes.

Natural History Museum

The skeletons of 20 dinosaurs and sea creatures are on display in the Natural History Museum's Dinosaur Hall.

California Science Center

Visitors to the science center can get a close-up view of the Space Shuttle *Endeavour* in its new home.

La Brea Tar Pits

The fossils of animals and plants that lived more than 10,000 years ago can be seen at the tar pits.

KEY WORDS

Research has shown that as much as 65 percent of all written material published in English is made up of 300 words. These 300 words cannot be taught using pictures or learned by sounding them out. They must be recognized by sight. This book contains 106 common sight words to help young readers improve their reading fluency and comprehension. This book also teaches young readers several important content words, such as proper nouns. These words are paired with pictures to aid in learning and improve understanding.

Page	Sight Words First Appearance
4	get, know, to
5	a, and, are, as, city, here, in, is, it, made, many, of, part, state, the, world
7	by, can, could, each, from, how, long, might, miles, other, places, take, there, these, use, where, which, you
8	about, days, has, more, only, they, trees, year
11	another, around, live, mountains, on, one, people, river, runs, through
12	before, began, came, different, first, group, move, named, our, over, time, up, was
15	at, come, food, often, shows, than, this
16	all, for, home, play, their
19	also, every, goods, important, while
20	found, land, now
21	later, opens
22	do, even, learn, most, must, picture, them, things
23	animals, be, close, its, new, plants, seen, that

Page	Content Words First Appearance
4	Los Angeles
5	California, capital, Hollywood, movies, television shows
7	highway, map, roads, Sacramento, trip
8	climate, fall, rain, spring, storm, wildflowers, winds, winter
11	area, coast, geography, Los Angeles River, Pacific Ocean, population, San Gabriel Mountains, United States
12	Aboriginal Peoples, families, Mexico, settlers, town
15	California Adventure, Disneyland, Hollywood Walk of Fame, person, rides, sidewalk, stars, theme parks, tourism, Universal Studios Hollywood, visitors
16	basketball, Chargers, Clippers, Dodgers, Dodger Stadium, football, Galaxy, games, hockey, Lakers, Rams, soccer, Sparks, sports, Staples Center, teams
19	economy, hotels, money, port, ship, souvenirs, trade
20	business, gold, settlement, timeline
21	construction, Los Angeles Municipal Airport, Los Angeles International Airport, Wizarding World of Harry Potter
22	Griffith Park Observatory, Moon, Sun, telescopes
23	California Science Center, dinosaurs, display, fossils, La Brea Tar Pits, Natural History Museum, sea creatures, skeletons, Space Shuttle *Endeavour*

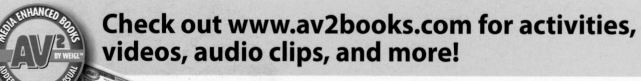